Look At Me

Look At Me

Written by Jamila White

P.O. Box 202
New York, NY 10276

white.jae@gmail.com
rualexmanagement@gmail.com

Library of Congress Cataloging-in-Publication Data
2015905913

Illustrated by Ana Zdravković

Dedication

This book is dedicated to my nieces,
nephews, godchildren and future children.
May you explore the World with open eyes
and may the heart of God lead and
guide you to know all truths.

To my mother Jocelyn A. Hicks thank you for your
patience and enduring love, you are irreplaceable.

"But when he, the Spirit of truth, comes, he will guide you into all
the truth. He will not speak on his own; he will speak only what he
hears, and he will tell you what is yet to come." John 16:13 NIV

Suddenly, the front door slammed. With tears in her eyes Kara came running toward her grandmother, who was knitting a blanket made of many colors.

"Grandma! Grandma!" yelled Kara.

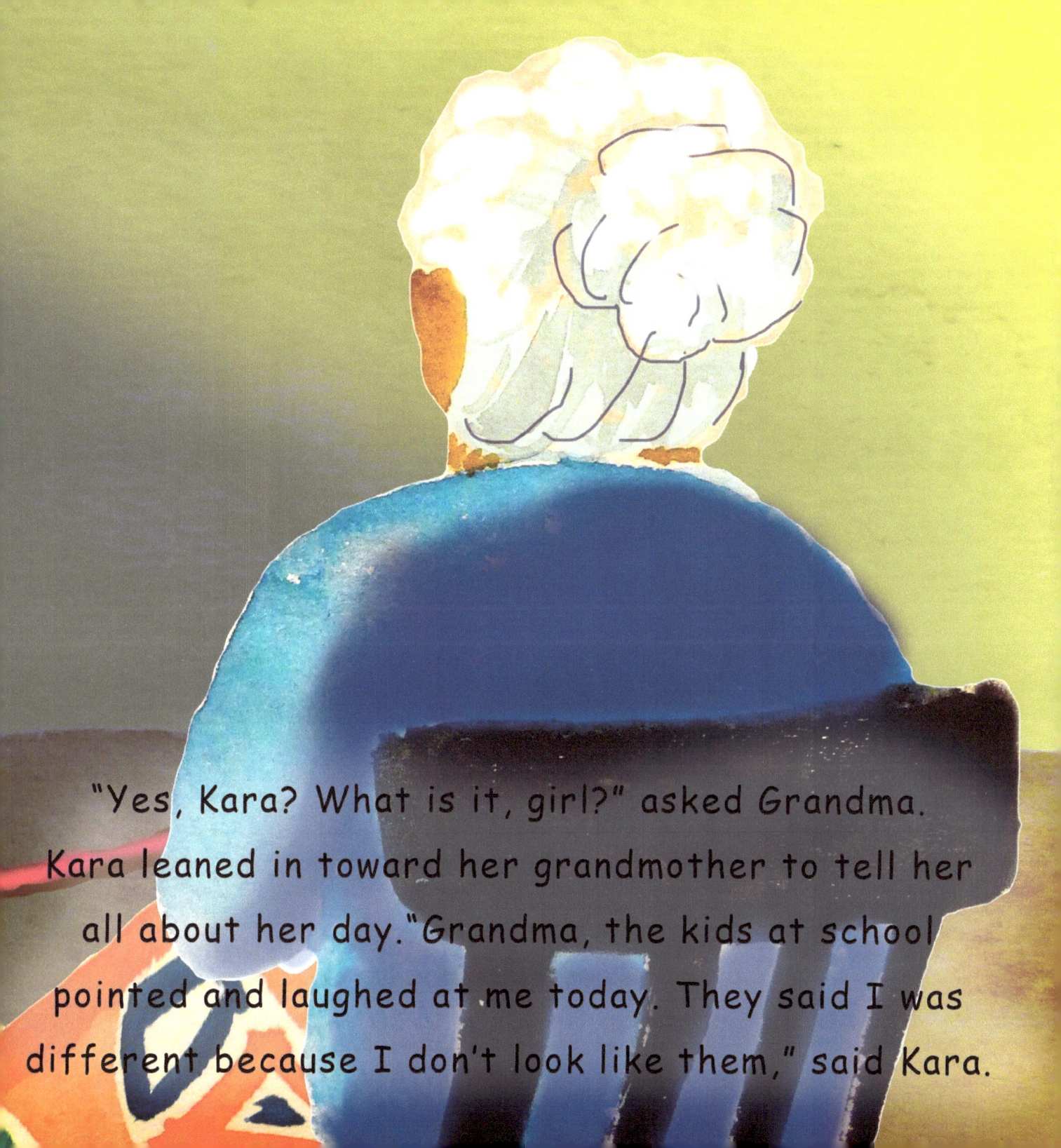

"Yes, Kara? What is it, girl?" asked Grandma. Kara leaned in toward her grandmother to tell her all about her day. "Grandma, the kids at school pointed and laughed at me today. They said I was different because I don't look like them," said Kara.

Grandma gently placed Kara on her lap and wiped the tears from her granddaughter's eyes.

"My darling Kara", said Grandma.

"You are different, and it's okay. In the eyes of God, we are all special." said Grandma.

"But what makes me special in the eyes
of God, Grandma?" asked Kara.

"What makes you special is that He sees your heart
and He knows it's full of love," said Grandma.

"Grandma, do you think God would mind if I didn't go to school tomorrow?" wondered Kara.

"I think God would mind. He would want you to go back to class and share with others the love He's shown you by forgiving those that have hurt you." said Grandma.

"Grandma, are you done with my blanket yet?" asked Kara.
"I am almost finished, child. Kara, you're not just one
color of the rainbow, you're many.

You have a heritage that stretches around the world.
The world is full of color and this blanket of many
colors is a rainbow of God's love for all people."
said Grandma.

"Grandma! I can't wait to share my blanket with the class on tomorrow. I want everyone to see why I love everything about me and why they should love everything about themselves too," said Kara.

"Kara, you'll have to wait until I finish the blanket, so hurry along," said Grandma.

As Kara happily danced to her room, she stopped in front of the mirror, daydreaming of all the people that would see her new blanket made of many colors.

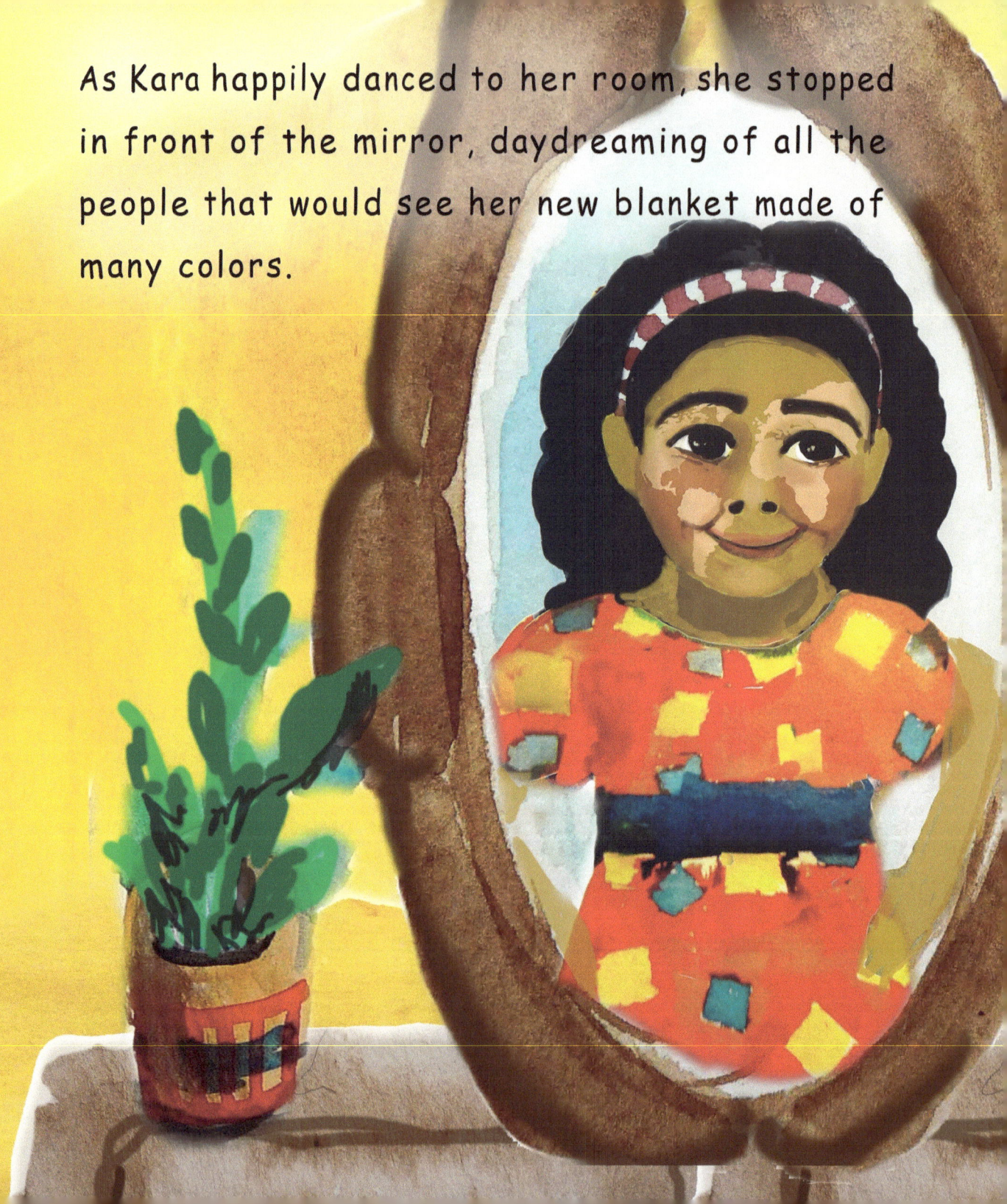

She sang,
"Look at me! For all the world to see,
I'm as happy as I can be.
I love everything about me."

As the song ended Kara's mom walked into the room.

"Kara, are you okay?" said Mom.

"Yes, Mom. I'm excited about my new blanket
made of many colors that Grandma is making
just for me," said Kara.

"I'm happy for you. I remember when Grandma made one just for me, like the one she's making for you. She told me many stories of how all the colors in the blanket were parts of my heritage."

Each color represented the history of my ancestors. Oh, how I loved my blanket made of many colors. And now you have one too," said Mom."

I can't wait until tomorrow, Mom, to show my blanket to everyone in my class," said Kara.

Mom chuckled to herself.
"My little girl, the dreamer."

Before you do anything else, please clean your room and come down to eat dinner," said Mom.

Mom left Kara to finish preparing dinner.

Kara continued to dance around
her room singing,
"Look at me! For all the world to see,
I'm happy
as I can be. I love
everything about me."

To Kara's surprise, her Dad saw her through the opening of her door. He came into her room with the food Mom had prepared for her.

"Kara, I heard you had a pretty rough start today," said Dad.

"I did, Dad. I understand now that when you're special people treat you differently," said Kara.

"It takes people time to get to know you and see how special you are. God is love and the love that's in Him is in you, and that makes you special. Tomorrow you will be able to share your blanket that was made with love," said Dad.

"Thanks, for everything Dad." said Kara.

"Okay, get ready for bed and sleep tight my sweet Kara," said Dad.

Dad kissed Kara on the forehead then closed the door while Kara fell fast asleep.

Kara awoke to the loud buzzing of her alarm. She quickly jumped out of bed to put on her clothes. Kara looked into the mirror and began to sing,

"Look at me! For all the world to see, I'm as happy as I can be. I love everything about me."

There was a knock at the door.

"Kara you're going to be late," said Dad from outside of Kara's door.

"Dad, today of all days, I must be perfect," said Kara.

"You're perfect in my eyes, Kara. You're beautiful and smart, and you will be late if you don't get on the bus," explained Dad.

"Okay," said Kara with a sigh.

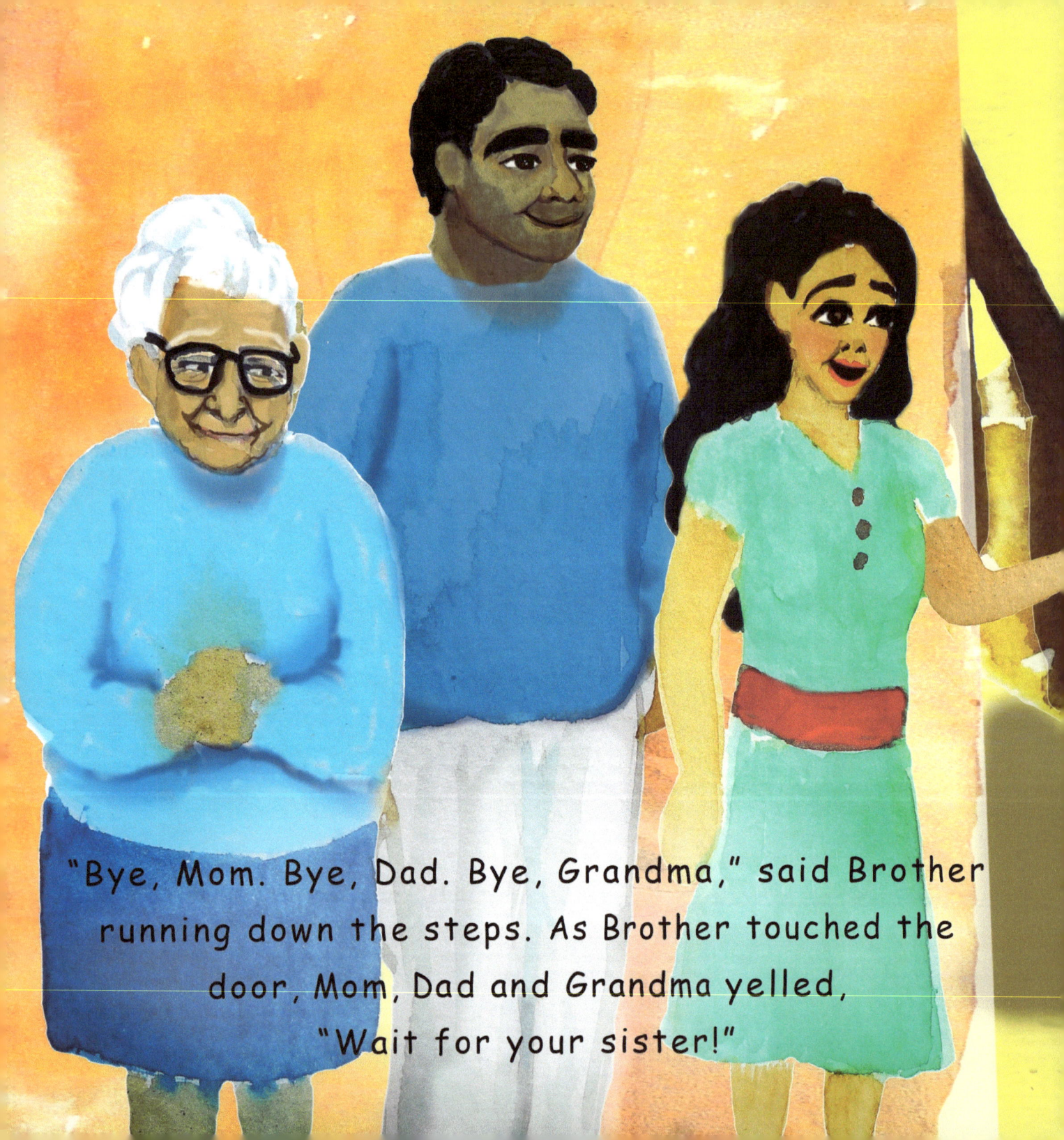

"Bye, Mom. Bye, Dad. Bye, Grandma," said Brother running down the steps. As Brother touched the door, Mom, Dad and Grandma yelled, "Wait for your sister!"

"She's going to make me late. I have to prepare for a test," said Brother.

"Son, please wait for your sister," said Dad.

"Kara, please hurry up! You're making us both late," said Brother.

Kara put on her backpack and walked out the door with her brother. Suddenly Kara remembered that she forgot the most important thing: her blanket!
She ran back into the house, grabbed the blanket, and kissed Grandma goodbye on the cheek.

Kara and Brother stepped on to the bus. "Brother, I can't wait to show everyone my blanket of many colors," said Kara.

"Oh, Kara, you have to stop talking about that blanket. There will be other things people will share that will be pretty cool to them," said Brother.

Brother then changed his seat to sit with his friends. When Brother moved seats on the bus, Kara felt all alone. While looking out the window, Kara wiped tears from her eyes. She began to sing, "Look at me! For all the world to see, I'm as happy as I can be. I love everything about me".

The Bus arrived at school. As the school bell rang, Ms. White, Kara's teacher stood in front of the class. "Good morning class. Today is a special day. It's 'Share My World' Day. I've asked each of you to bring in a special item that will show your family history. All of us have a unique heritage that brings an assortment of color and style that your classmates are unaware of. Today, I've asked Kara to present first," said Ms. White.

"Thank you, Ms. White," said Kara. "My blanket is made of many colors for all of you to see.

My grandmother tells me that we are all special in the eyes of God. He sees only the color of love. Love is what the world is made of, and that makes you no different from me," said Kara.

Kara continued, telling her classmates that the blanket

is a part of their heritage as well. With excitement in

their eyes, Kara's classmates ran up to look at the

blanket closely.

Then, to her surprise, Kara saw her family standing outside
of the classroom door.
"You all came to see me present at Share My World
Day!" exclaimed Kara.
"We wouldn't have missed you sharing a part of
us too," said Mom.

"I was able to finish my test early," said Brother.

"Baby girl, you did well today,"
said Dad.

"I'm proud of you. Today you made my heart glad
because you shared with the world the blanket
made of many colors that I made just for you.
It has brought us all closer together through
God's love for all people",
said Grandmother.

Kara hugged them tightly.
"Look at me! For all the
world to see, I'm as
happy as I can be. I love
everything about me.
For God so loved the world
that He made you and me,"
sang Kara.

The End

www.ingramcontent.com/pod-product-compliance
Lightning Source LLC
Chambersburg PA
CBHW042059040426
42448CB00002B/67